D'Nealian® Handwriting

3

Written by Donald Neal Thurber

Scott Foresman
is an imprint of

PEARSON

Editorial Offices: Glenview, Illinois • Parsippany, New Jersey • New York, New York
Sales Offices: Boston, Massachusetts • Duluth, Georgia • Glenview, Illinois • Coppell, Texas
Sacramento, California • Mesa, Arizona

Acknowledgments

Illustrations

Lois Axeman 22, 34, 35, 37, 40, 55; Kenneth Batelman 85; Karen Stormer Brooks 35, 119; Leslie Bowman 19; Judith dufour-Love 25, 26, 27, 31; Lane Gregory 56, 45, 70, 119; Konrad Hock 102, 103, 107, 108; Gary Hoover 85; Cheryl Kirk-Noll 18, 21, 50; Richard Kriegler 114; Yoshi Miyake 52, 53, 72, 82, 83, 121; James Needham 12, 13, 14, 15; Jan Spivey Gilchrist 73; Judy Sakaguchi 23; Cindy Salans-Rosenheim 86; Lauren Scheuer 73, 99; Carol Schwartz 16, 17; Jeff Severn 8, Lena Shiffman 80, 81; Georgia Shola 9, 59, 110, 111; Susan Swan 33; Andrea Tachiera 66, 67, 69, 104, 105; Jenny Vainisl 39; Dana Verkouteren 99; Jack Wallen 28; Darcy Whitehead 3, 4, 5, 11, 29, 49, 57, 58, 73, 77, 78, 79, 124

Photographs

Every effort has been made to secure permission and provide appropriate credit for photographic material. The publisher deeply regrets any omission and pledges to correct errors call to its attention in subsequent editions.

Unless otherwise acknowledged, all photographs are the property of Scott Foresman, a division of Pearson Education.

Photo locators denoted as follows: Top (T), Center (C), Bottom (B), Left (L), Right (R), Backaground (Bkgd).

42 ©Bronwyn Photo/Fotolia.com; **43** ©Kzenon/Fotolia.com; **47(l-r)** ©Wojciech Gajda/Fotolia.com; ©Paylessimages/Fotolia.com; ©Stanisa Martinovic/Fotolia.com; **61** ©Igor Zhorov/Fotolia.com; **62** ©clearviewstock/Fotolia.com; **63** ©nsphotography/Fotolia.com; **88** ©Ayeshar/Fotolia.com; **89** ©Ina van Hateren/Fotolia.com; **91** ©Scott Prokop/Fotolia.com; **92** ©Bill Perry/Fotolia.com; **93** ©michael langley/Fotolia.com; **95(l-r)** ©Michael Holst/Fotolia.com; ©tomas del amo/Fotolia.com; ©Jennifer LaFleur/Fotolia.com; ©Maridav/Fotolia.com; **97** ©auremar/Fotolia.com; **112** ©Supermurmel/Fotolia.com; **113** ©Photo Courtesy of NASA; **115** ©Photo Courtesy of NASA; **122** ©DerSchmock/Fotolia.com.

D'Nealian® Handwriting is a registered trademark of Donald Neal Thurber

ISBN-13: 978-0-328-21199-9
ISBN-10: 0-328-21199-0

24   17

Table of Contents

Unit Four Writing Capital Cursive Letters

Unit One

Getting Ready to Write

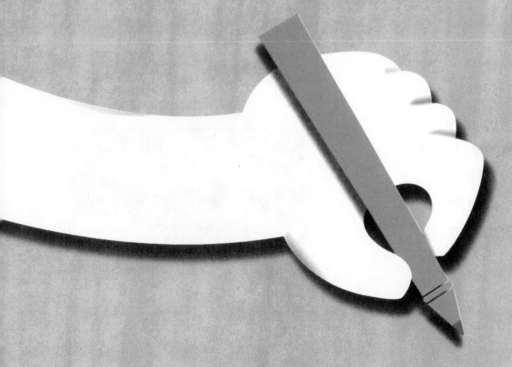

Left-handed Position for Writing

Sit tall with both feet on the floor. Rest both arms on your desk.

Your paper should slant from the right at the top to the left at the bottom. Rest your right hand on the paper to hold it in place.

Hold the pencil lightly between your thumb and index finger. Look at the picture to see how. The eraser end of the pencil should point toward your left shoulder.

Right-handed Position for Writing

Sit tall with both feet on the floor. Rest both arms on your desk.

Your paper should slant from the left at the top to the right at the bottom. Rest your left hand on the paper to hold it in place.

Hold the pencil lightly between your thumb and index finger. Look at the picture to see how. The eraser end of the pencil should point toward your right shoulder.

Letter Size and Form

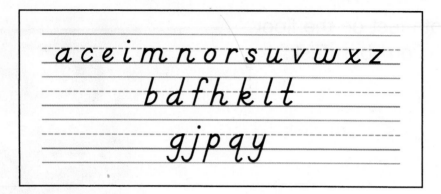

Manuscript letters have only three sizes. There are small letters, tall letters, and letters with descenders.

Small letters sit on the bottom line. They touch the middle line. Write three small letters.

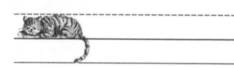

Tall letters also sit on the bottom line. They touch the top line. Write three tall letters.

Letters with descenders are **g, j, p, q,** and **y.** These letters have tails that go down under the bottom line. The descenders touch the line below. Write three letters with descenders.

Forming letters correctly helps make handwriting easy to read. Some letters, like **b, d, o,** and **g,** must be closed. The letters **t** and **f** must be crossed. Dot the letters **i** and **j.**

Can you read the phrase below?

The phrase is **biggest dog.** Why is it so hard to read?

Write the phrase **biggest dog** correctly.

Is your phrase easier to read?

8

Letter Slant and Spacing

Slant all your letters the same way. That will make your handwriting easier to read. Find the slant that is right for you. Then keep that slant.

Some writers slant their letters to the right.

Some writers slant their letters to the left.

right

left

Some writers make their letters straight up and down.

Do not slant your letters different ways.

up and down

different

Which handwriting is hard to read? Why is it hard?

Spacing is important. Letters and words should not be too close together or too far apart. Write this sentence. Use correct spacing.

Letme   outo fhere!

Let me out of here!

9

Cursive Is Coming

People may write messages, lists, and other information in two ways. Read the two lists below. Some letters look almost the same in both lists.

A letter is circled in each list that looks almost the same. Circle three more letters that look almost the same in cursive and in manuscript.

Manuscript
You already know how to write like this.

Cursive
You will soon learn how to write like this.

Ms. Jensen's Class
Favorite Pets

cat
dog
hamster
fish
bird

Ms. Jensen's Class
Favorite Pets

cat
dog
hamster
fish
bird

Unit Two

Reviewing Manuscript Letters

Using Numbers in a List

Mrs. Matoba's class is having a pet show. Write in manuscript the list of pets entered in the show. Line up all the numbers in the list. Follow each number with a period.

Pet Show

1. Mittens	6. Dudley
2. Casey	7. Spot
3. Felix	8. Buttons
4. Gus	9. Muffy
5. Bingo	10. Dusty

Writing Manuscript aA, dD, oO, and gG

Write the lower-case letters.

a a a a   a

d   d

o   o

g   g

Write the capital letters.

A A A   D D D   O O O   G G G

Write the names.

Great Dane

Atlas Dog Obedience

Writing Manuscript cC, eE, and sS

Write the lower-case letters.

c c

e e

s s

Write the capital letters.

C E S

Write the names.

Cocker Spaniel

Edgar's Dog Grooming

Old English Sheepdog

Writing Manuscript fF, bB, and lL

Write the lower-case letters.

f   f

b   b

l   l

Write the capital letters.

F   B   L

Write the names.

Libby

Fluffy

Barkley

Lassie

Fido's Biscuits

Writing Manuscript tT, hH, and kK

Happy Trails Kennel

Write the lower-case letters.

t   t

h   h

k   k

Write the capital letters.

T   H   K

Write the names and the sentence.

King

Tuffy

Take Heidi to the Happy Trails Kennel.

Writing Manuscript iI, uU, wW, and yY

Write the lower-case letters.

i   *i*

u   *u*

w   *w*

y   *y*

Write the capital letters.

I   *U*   *W*   *Y*

Write the sentence.

Yes, Uncle Willie and I saw a cute puppy.

17

Writing Manuscript jJ, rR, nN, mM, and pP

Write the lower-case letters.

j   j

r   r

n   n

m   m

p   p

Write the capital letters.

J   R   N

M   P

Write the sentence.

Poodles run and jump.

Writing Manuscript qQ, vV, zZ, and xX

Write the lower-case letters.

q   q

v   v

z   z

x   x

Write the capital letters.

Q   V   Z   X

Write the sentence.

Liz and Xavier McQueen pose with Max and Zeus.

Practice

Write the lower-case manuscript letters
in alphabetical order.

a b c d e f g h i
j k l m n o p q r
s t u v w x y z

Write the capital manuscript letters in
alphabetical order.

A B C D E F G
H I J K L M N
O P Q R S T U
V W X Y Z

Review

Write the words.

tub

_____

- - - - - - - - - - - - -

_____

Pixie
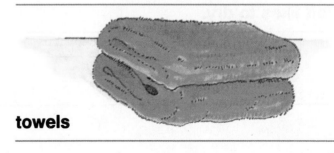

_____

- - - - - - - - - - - - -

_____

soap

_____

- - - - - - - - - - - - -

_____

puppy

_____

- - - - - - - - - - - - -

_____

Gloria

_____

- - - - - - - - - - - - -

_____

brushes

_____

- - - - - - - - - - - - -

_____

Jeff

_____

- - - - - - - - - - - - -

_____

towels

_____

- - - - - - - - - - - - -

_____

21

Evaluation

Write the words and sentences.

Dog Washing Today

Remember: Slant all your letters the same way.

Zack will shampoo.

Rinse the puppy quickly.

Jeff likes to dry.

Check Your Handwriting
Do all your letters slant the same way?

Yes   No
☐   ☐

22

Making a Schedule

The Harrises are going away for the weekend. Sarah will take care of their dog, Gus, while they are away. Mrs. Harris made a schedule to help Sarah remember what to do.

8:00 A.M.	Walk Gus and feed him breakfast. Give him fresh water.
1:00 P.M.	Take Gus for a walk. Play fetch.
6:00 P.M.	Feed Gus dinner. Brush him and walk him.
9:00 P.M.	Walk Gus. Give him a dog treat. Say good night.

Copy the schedule. Write as straight across as you can even though there are no writing lines on the schedule. Be sure to adjust the size of your handwriting to fit the space.

Here's Cursive

You know how to write manuscript letters. Now you will learn to write cursive letters. What types of writing will you do in cursive?

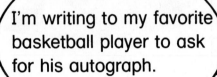

I'm writing to my favorite basketball player to ask for his autograph.

I'm practicing my signature for signing autographs when I'm famous.

Two Ways to Write

Look closely at the two sentences below. One is in manuscript, and the other is in cursive. Circle the letters that look almost the same in manuscript and cursive. Most cursive letters are joined together. Make a ‿ under five places where the letters are joined. The first one is done for you.

Manuscript

I like

cursive.

Cursive

I like

cursive.

Strokes That Make Cursive Letters

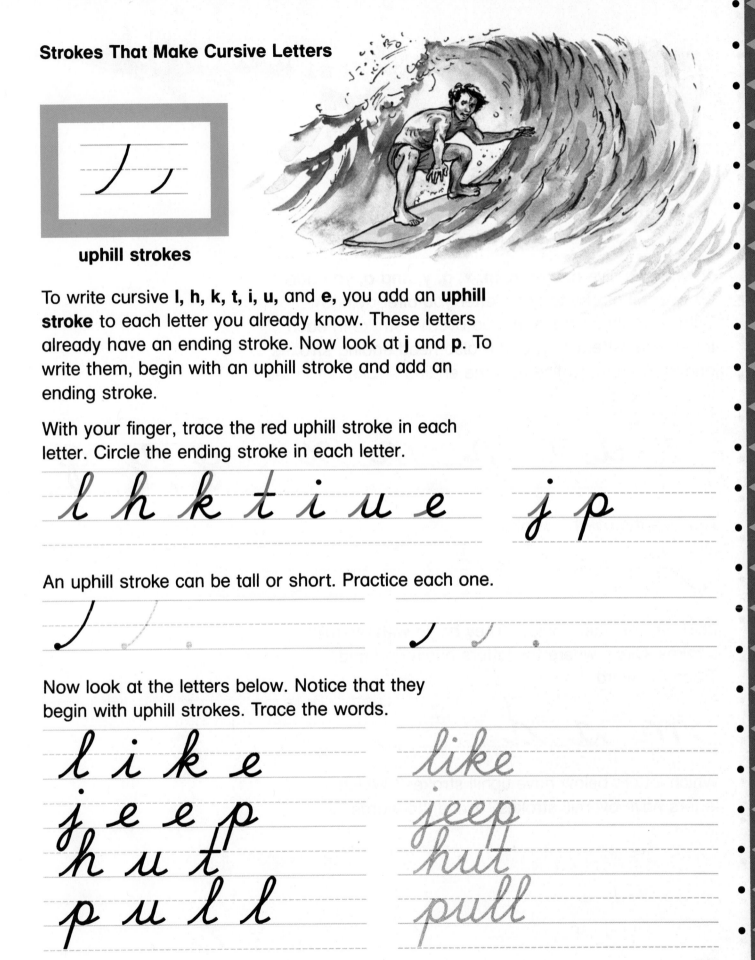

uphill strokes

To write cursive **l, h, k, t, i, u,** and **e,** you add an **uphill stroke** to each letter you already know. These letters already have an ending stroke. Now look at **j** and **p**. To write them, begin with an uphill stroke and add an ending stroke.

With your finger, trace the red uphill stroke in each letter. Circle the ending stroke in each letter.

l h k t i u e   j p

An uphill stroke can be tall or short. Practice each one.

Now look at the letters below. Notice that they begin with uphill strokes. Trace the words.

like   like
jeep   jeep
hut   hut
pull   pull

25

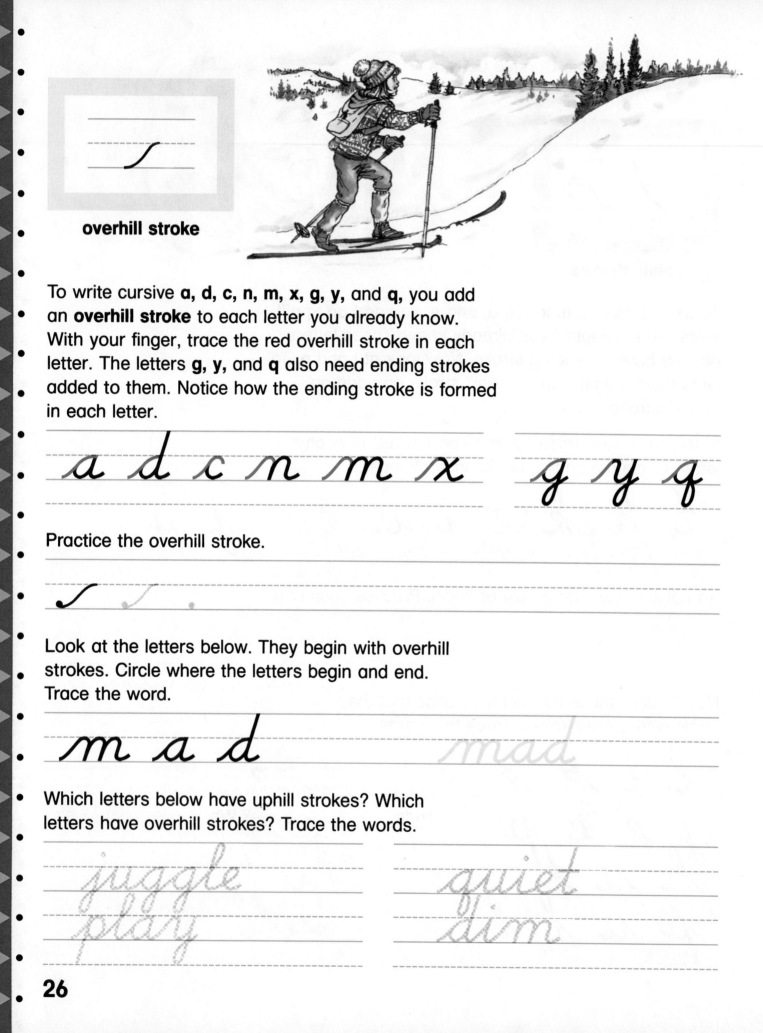

overhill stroke

To write cursive **a, d, c, n, m, x, g, y,** and **q,** you add an **overhill stroke** to each letter you already know. With your finger, trace the red overhill stroke in each letter. The letters **g, y,** and **q** also need ending strokes added to them. Notice how the ending stroke is formed in each letter.

Practice the overhill stroke.

Look at the letters below. They begin with overhill strokes. Circle where the letters begin and end. Trace the word.

Which letters below have uphill strokes? Which letters have overhill strokes? Trace the words.

sidestroke

The letters **o, w,** and **b** end with a **sidestroke.** Which letter begins with an overhill stroke? Which two letters begin with uphill strokes? With your finger, trace the red sidestroke in each letter.

Practice the sidestroke.

Look at the letters below. Notice where they begin and end. A sidestroke letter always joins the following letter near the middle line. This changes the beginning stroke of the following letter. Notice how the sidestroke changes **n, e,** and **a** in **on, wet,** and **bat.** Trace the words.

o n *w e t* *b a t*

on *wet* *bat*

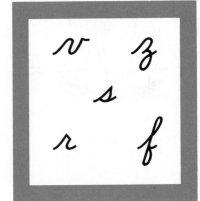

The letters **v, z, s, r,** and **f** are special because they look different from the letters you already know. Which letter ends with a sidestroke? Which two letters begin with overhill strokes? Which three letters begin with uphill strokes? Trace the letters **v, z, s, r,** and **f.**

v v z z s s r r f f

The words below have all of the joining strokes you learned. Find five letters that begin with **uphill strokes.** Find four letters that begin with **overhill strokes.** Find three letters that end with **sidestrokes.** Then trace the words.

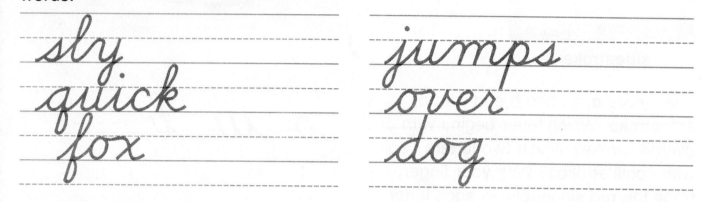

sly
quick
fox

jumps
over
dog

Read the following sentences.

I am ready to write in cursive. Are you?

Hey, you're that New Kid aren't you ?

Unit Three

Writing Lower-case Cursive Letters

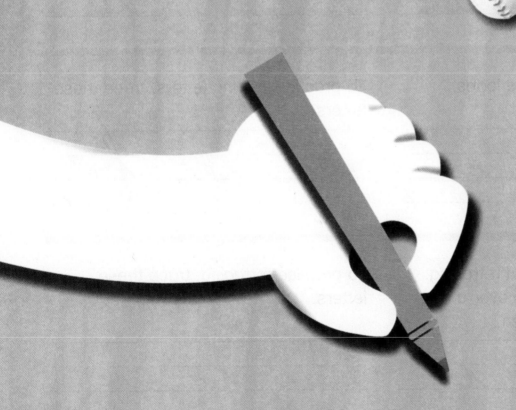

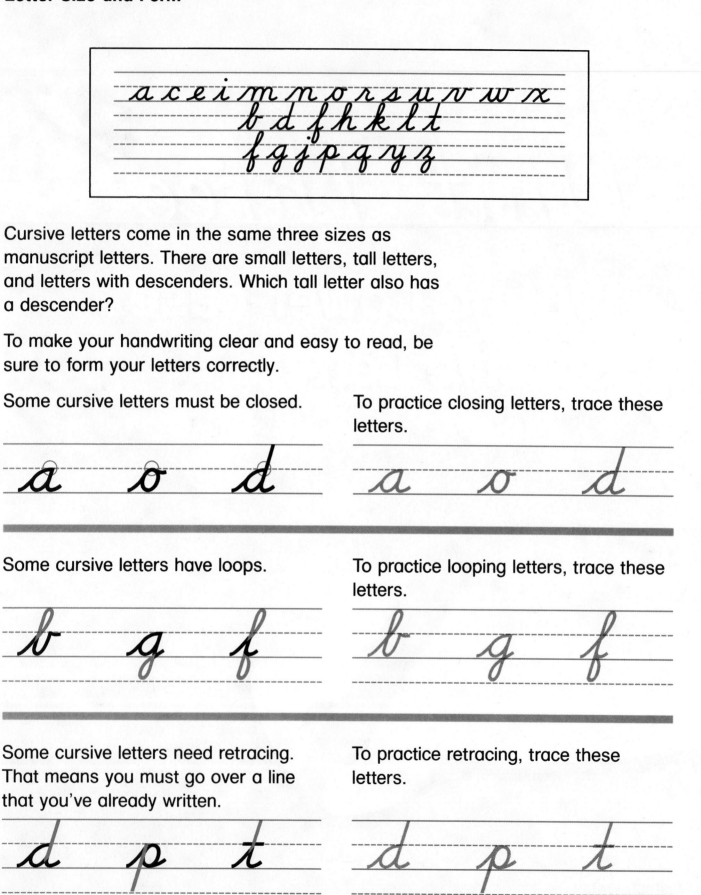

Cursive letters come in the same three sizes as manuscript letters. There are small letters, tall letters, and letters with descenders. Which tall letter also has a descender?

To make your handwriting clear and easy to read, be sure to form your letters correctly.

Some cursive letters must be closed.

To practice closing letters, trace these letters.

Some cursive letters have loops.

To practice looping letters, trace these letters.

Some cursive letters need retracing. That means you must go over a line that you've already written.

To practice retracing, trace these letters.

Letter Slant and Word Spacing

When you write in cursive, slant all your letters the same way. You may slant your letters to the right or to the left. You may write them straight up and down. Do not slant your letters different ways.

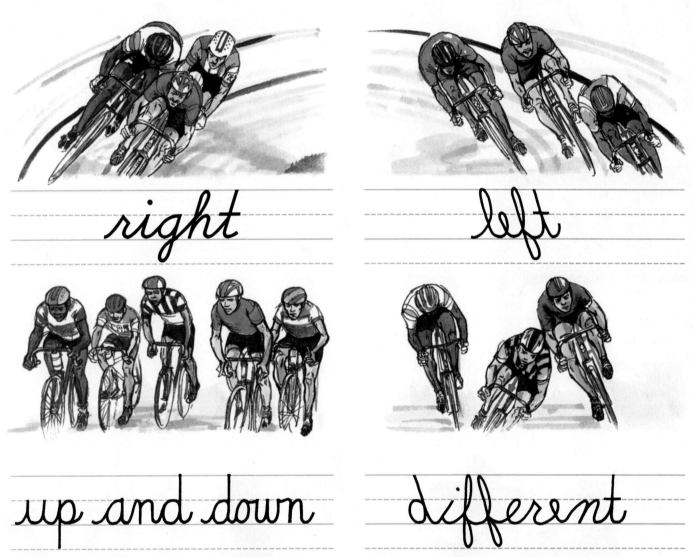

right

left

up and down

different

Which writing is hard to read? Why is it hard?

Use correct spacing when you write. The letters in a word should be evenly spaced. Leave more space between words than between letters in a word.

aredbike   *a red bike*

Which writing is easier to read? Why is it easier?

Writing Cursive l, h, k, and t

Cursive letters **l**, **h**, **k**, and **t** look like their manuscript forms. Add an uphill stroke to write the cursive letter. Trace and write the letters.

l l   *l l.*   *l*

h h   *h h.*   *h*

k k   *k k.*   *k*

t t   *t t.*   *t*

Amy has a collection of letters. Write each letter in cursive.

l   h   k   t

When you write in cursive, you join the letters. Most letters join at the bottom line. Trace and write the joined letters.

ll   ll   ll
lh   lh   lh
lk   lk   lk
lt   lt   lt
hh   hh   hh
hl   hl   hl
ht   ht   ht
kl   kl   kl
tt   tt   tt
tl   tl   tl
th   th   th

kite   hut   lei   tree

Writing Cursive i, u, and e

Cursive letters **i**, **u**, and **e** look like their manuscript forms. Add an uphill stroke to write the cursive letter. Trace and write the letters.

Trace and write the words.

it

it

hull

hull

let

let

hi

hi

kite

kite

tell

tell

Trace and write the words and phrases.

hit

hit

hut

hut

hill

hill

lei

lei

tie

tie

till

till

like the hike

like the hike

the little ukulele

the little ukulele

Writing Cursive j and p

Cursive letters **j** and **p** look very much like their manuscript forms. To write them in cursive, you must add an uphill stroke <u>and</u> an ending stroke. Trace and write the letters.

Trace and write the words.

jet

jet

pet

pet

peek

peek

up

up

help

help

keep

keep

Review

Write the words.

hill

hut

jeep

jet

lei

pup

ukulele

kite

Evaluation

Remember: Cross the letter **t** and dot the letters **i** and **j**.

Write the phrases.

the hike uphill

like the jeep

the little hut

kept the pup

Check Your Handwriting

	Yes	No
Did you cross the letter **t**?	☐	☐
Did you dot the letters **i** and **j**?	☐	☐

40

Trace and write the phrases.

a little child

a little child

the path ahead

the path ahead

packed a peach

packed a peach

the apple juice

the apple juice

43

Writing Cursive n, m, and x

Cursive letters **n, m,** and **x** look like their manuscript forms. Add an overhill stroke to write the cursive letter. Trace and write the letters.

n m

n n.   *n*

m m

m m.   *m*

x x

x x.   *x*

Trace and write the words.

can

can

ham

ham

lunch

lunch

taxi

taxi

milk

milk

meat

meat

Trace and write the phrases.

lettuce and pickle

lettuce and pickle

mixed the chicken

mixed the chicken

the next picnic

the next picnic

elm and maple

elm and maple

Writing Cursive g, y, and q

Cursive letters **g**, **y**, and **q** look like their manuscript forms. To write them in cursive, you must add an overhill stroke <u>and</u> an ending stroke. Trace and write the letters.

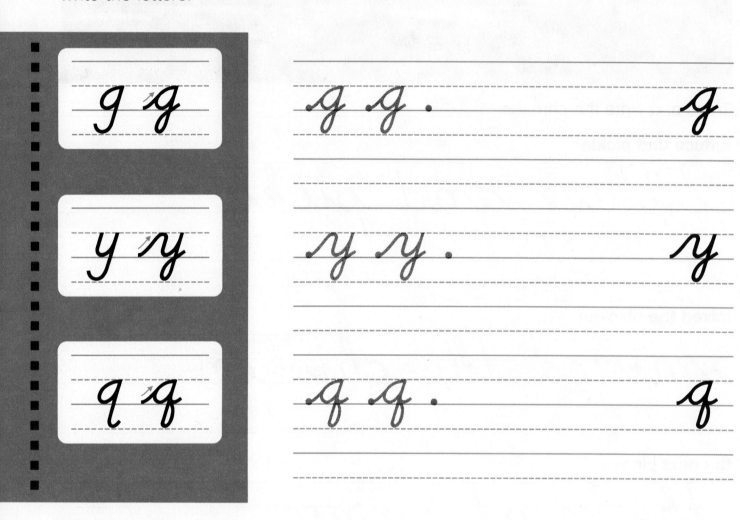

Trace and write the words.

my

my

quit

quit

light

light

Review

Write the words and phrases.

picnic

game

taxi

ham

a quacking duck

a yellow kitten

49

Evaluation

Remember: Descenders should touch the line below.

Write the phrases.

the next meal

a picnic at night

hugging a child

the cuddly quilt

Check Your Handwriting

Do your descenders touch the line below?

Yes No

☐ ☐

Writing a Postcard

There is very little space on a postcard. You must write small, form your letters clearly, and keep your lines straight. Manuscript is often clearer than cursive when you have to write small.

When you address an envelope or a postcard, use all capital manuscript letters and no punctuation marks. Abbreviate words like *Street* and *Apartment*, and the name of the state.

Dear Kathy,
    We are having lots of fun camping. Yesterday we hiked around the lake. Today we went swimming. Later, Dad and I caught some fish.
                Your friend,
                Jean Anne

MISS KATHRYN SCHULTZ
501 FARGO ST APT 320
CHICAGO IL 60626

Copy the postcard in manuscript.

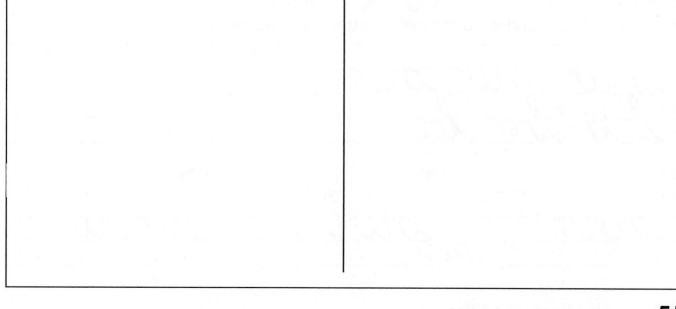

Writing Cursive o, w, and b

You can see manuscript **o** and **w** in cursive **o** and **w**.
Cursive **b** looks very much like manuscript **b**. Begin
cursive **o** with an overhill stroke. Begin cursive **w** and **b**
with an uphill stroke. Each letter ends with a sidestroke
near the middle line. Trace and write the letters.

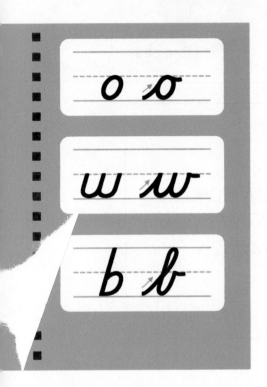

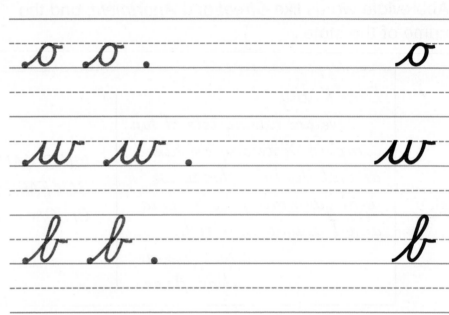

Remember that **o, w,** and **b** join the next letter near the
middle line. This changes the beginning stroke of the
next letter. Trace and write the joined letters and words.

ow ow ow
bo bo bo

bow

bow

owl

owl

wow

wow

Review

Write the words and the phrase.

wallet

book

boot

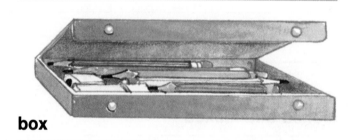

box

belt

watch

an old blue bike

Evaluation

Remember: Most letters in words are joined at the bottom line. The letters **o, w,** and **b** join the next letter near the middle line.

Write the phrases.

my new black and yellow notebook

looked and looked

below the window

Check Your Handwriting

Are the letters in your words joined correctly?

Yes ☐   No ☐

56

Review

Write the words and the phrase.

wallet

_____

_____

book

_____

_____

boot

_____

_____

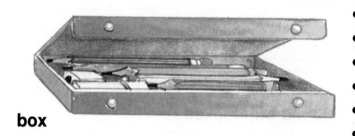

box

_____

_____

belt

_____

_____

watch

_____

_____

an old blue bike

_____

_____

55

Evaluation

Remember: Most letters in words are joined at the bottom line. The letters **o, w,** and **b** join the next letter near the middle line.

Write the phrases.

my new black and yellow notebook

looked and looked

below the window

Check Your Handwriting

Are the letters in your words joined correctly?

Yes ☐ No ☐

Making a List

Mrs. Jordan's class made a list of the items in the Lost and Found. They put the list on the bulletin board in the hall where everyone could see it. Copy the items on the list. Use cursive handwriting. Plan your space so that each item fits on one line. Make sure your sidestroke letters are joined correctly.

Lost and Found

one black boot   a ballpoint pen
one pink mitten   one yellow pencil
a yellow wool hat   a pink notebook
a new book   an old watch
a ball and mitt   a blue coat

Making a Poster

Liz and Marta made a poster to tell people about the Lincoln School Book Fair. They wanted to tell the time, the date, and the place. This is how it looked.

Copy the poster in manuscript handwriting. Be sure to write larger than you usually do.

Book Fair
Friday, May 17
10:00 A.M. to 3:00 P.M.
Lincoln School Gym
Come to the Fair!

Writing Titles and Authors

These are some of the books the third-graders bought at the Book Fair. Write the titles and authors in manuscript. Be sure to leave enough space between words, and underline a title when you write it.

<u>A Chair for My Mother</u> by Vera B. Williams

<u>Zeely</u> by Virginia Hamilton

<u>Where the Buffaloes Begin</u> by Olaf Baker

<u>Owls in the Family</u> by Farley Mowat

Writing Cursive v and z

Cursive **v** and **z** do not look like manuscript **v** and **z**.
Notice that cursive **v** ends with a sidestroke. Trace
and write the letters.

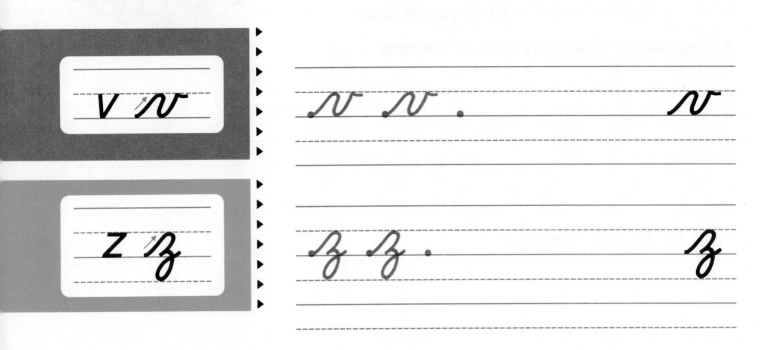

Remember that **v** joins the next letter near the
middle line. Trace and write the words.

violin

violin

move

move

van

van

buzz

buzz

lazy

lazy

zip

zip

Trace and write the phrases.

a lovely event

a lovely event

a lazy, hazy evening

a lazy, hazy evening

a dozen people

a dozen people

lively jazz

lively jazz

Writing Cursive s and r

Cursive **s** and **r** do not look like manuscript **s** and **r**.
Trace and write the letters.

Trace and write the words.

strings

strings

sing

sing

songs

songs

rhythm

rhythm

Trace and write the phrases.

rock and roll

rock and roll

orchestra and chorus

orchestra and chorus

seven percussion instruments

seven percussion instruments

a crazy rhythm

a crazy rhythm

Writing Cursive f

Cursive **f** does not look like its manuscript form.
Trace and write the letter.

Trace and write the words and phrases.

fun

fun

fast

fast

first

first

treble clef

treble clef

bass clef

bass clef

Trace and write the phrases.

four friends on flutes

four friends on flutes

a good effort

a good effort

friendly faces

friendly faces

my favorite music

my favorite music

Joining Sidestroke Letters

The letters **o, w, b,** and **v** must join the next letter near the middle line. This changes the beginning stroke of the next letter. Trace and write the joined letters and words.

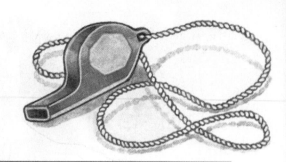

ba ba ba

tuba

ol ol ol

piccolo

wa wa wa

walk

bl bl bl

blue

or or or

uniform

wh wh wh

whistle

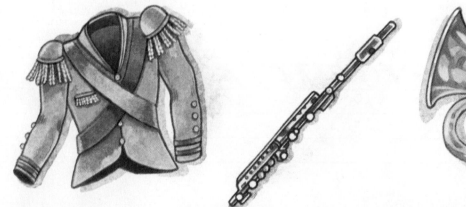

Trace and write the joined letters and words.

bu bu bu
bus
vi vi vi
viola
ov ov ov
ve ve ve
glove
ob ob ob
bo bo bo
oboe
oo oo oo
on on on
bassoon
om om om
trombone

Practice

Write the letters.

Circle your best letter in each line.

Practice joining these letters.

vi

st

sa

sh

fr

zz

68

Review

Write the words.

zither

harp

drums

violin

recorder

trumpet

saxophone

flute

Evaluation

Remember: Small letters should touch the middle line.

Write the phrases.

a symphony orchestra

----

lovely zither music

----

five pieces for the violin

Check Your Handwriting

Do your small letters touch the middle line?

Yes ☐   No ☐

Writing Number Words and Time

Write the number words in cursive handwriting.
Remember to dot the letter **i** and cross the letter **t**.

zero

one

two

three

four

five

six

seven

eight

nine

ten

Beginning band practice is at 9:00, advanced band
practice is at 1:00, and chorus practice is at 3:00.
Write the times in numbers and words. Make sure your
numbers are the same size as your tall letters.

9:00   **nine o'clock**

1:00   **one o'clock**

3:00   **three o'clock**

Writing Number Words

An orchestra is made up of many instruments. Write the number and names of the instruments in the orchestra below. Make sure you form your letters clearly and make them the correct size.

twelve violins

_____

- -

_____

five cellos

_____

- -

_____

four flutes

_____

- -

_____

six clarinets

_____

- -

_____

two trumpets

_____

- -

_____

three drums

_____

- -

Writing a Language Arts Test

Good handwriting helps you do well on language arts tests. Good handwriting makes your written answers easy to read. Good handwriting helps you communicate your ideas more clearly.

Getting Ready
- Read the prompt carefully.
- Think about what the prompt asks you to do.
- Write down key words from the prompt to help you stay focused on the topic.

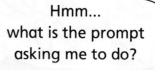

Hmm... what is the prompt asking me to do?

Writing a Narrative
- Use key words to keep your focus on the topic.
- Write a good beginning with a fact or question that engages readers.
- Support the topic with details that tell more about the people or events you are writing about.
- Write a strong ending.
- Use your best handwriting.

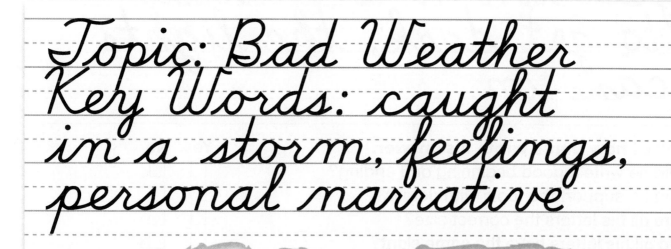

Topic: Bad Weather
Key Words: caught in a storm, feelings, personal narrative

- Review and edit your writing. Use proofreading marks to make changes or erase carefully and rewrite.

Here is a writing prompt and Derek's answer.

We all live with bad weather sometimes. Think about a time you were caught in a rain, wind, or snowstorm. What happened? What feelings did you have? Write a personal narrative to describe your experience.

Last year my brother and I were ~~were~~ at home during a bad snowstorm. We felt happy because school was closed! But, we were scared because ~~becus~~ we had no lights. But, just when it started to get dark, the lights came on.

Look at how Derek wrote his answer.

	Yes	No
• Did he write a good beginning and ending?	☐	☐
• Did he support the topic with details?	☐	☐
• Are all his letters the correct size?	☐	☐
• Do all his letters have the same slant?	☐	☐
• Did he fix his mistakes carefully?	☐	☐

Circle words or letters that do not have the correct slant.
Make a line under letters that are not the correct size.

Now you write a response to the same prompt that Derek used.

_____

_____

_____

_____

_____

_____

_____

_____

_____

_____

_____

_____

_____

_____

Check your handwriting.   Yes   No

- Did you write a good beginning and ending?   ☐   ☐
- Did you support the topic with details?   ☐   ☐
- Are all your letters the correct size?   ☐   ☐
- Do your letters have the same slant?   ☐   ☐
- Did you fix your mistakes carefully?   ☐   ☐
- Is your handwriting easy to read?   ☐   ☐

Put a check mark next to the sentence that you think is written best.

Writing Numbers in a Paragraph

Write out a number at the beginning of a sentence.
Write out numbers that are one or two words.

> Six hundred twenty students go to
> Hoffman School. Eighty-two are in beginning
> band, seventy-three are in advanced band, and
> ninety-seven are in chorus.

Copy the paragraph below. Use manuscript writing.
Remember to indent the first line.

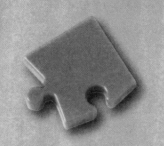

Unit Four

Writing Capital Cursive Letters

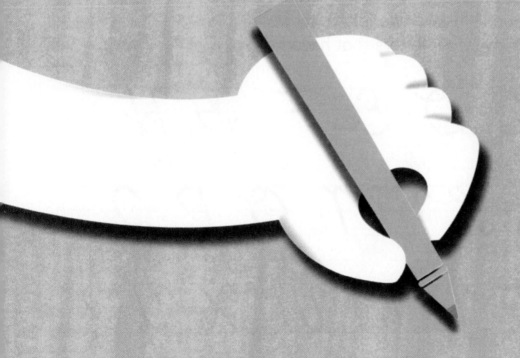

Letter Size and Form

Capital cursive letters all touch the top and bottom lines. Three capital letters also have descenders that touch the line below. To make your handwriting clear and easy to read, be sure to form your letters correctly.

Some capital letters must be closed.

A P

Some capital letters have loops.

D L

You must retrace when you write some capital letters. That means you must go over a line you've already written.

B N

Some capital letters have descenders. The descenders should touch the line below.

J Y

Look at the capital letters in the alphabet below. Circle four letters that must be closed. Underline five letters that have loops. Put a ✔ above two letters that have descenders. Put an **X** over four letters that have retracing.

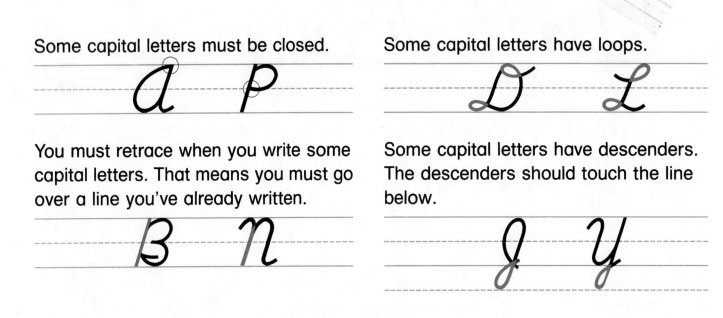

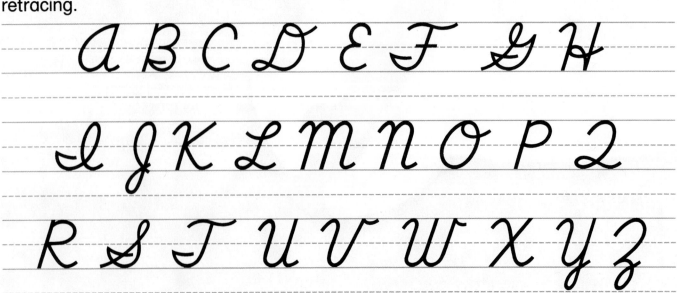

Letter Slant

Slant your capital letters in the same direction that you slant your lower-case letters. You may slant your letters to the right or to the left. You may write them straight up and down. Do not slant your capital letters differently from your lower-case letters.

Right   *Left*

Up and down   *Different*

Which writing is hard to read? Why is it hard?

Numbers and punctuation marks should slant in the same direction as your letters. Look at this sentence written two ways. Circle four letters that slant the wrong way in the first sentence. Then trace the correct sentence.

Will you come to lunch at 12:00?

Will you come to lunch at 12:00?

Write this phrase. Slant all your letters the same way.

the same slant

Do your letters all slant the same way?   Yes ☐   No ☐

Writing Cursive A and C

Capital cursive **A** looks different from manuscript **A**. Cursive **C** looks like its manuscript form. Trace and write the letters.

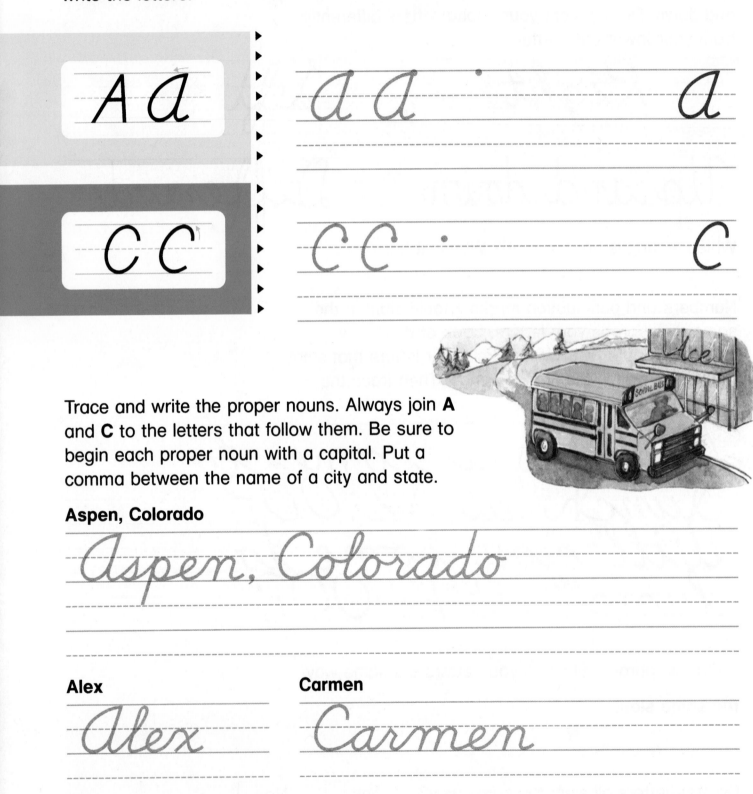

Trace and write the proper nouns. Always join **A** and **C** to the letters that follow them. Be sure to begin each proper noun with a capital. Put a comma between the name of a city and state.

Aspen, Colorado

Aspen, Colorado

Alex

Alex

Carmen

Carmen

Trace and write the sentences.

Anne's class visited Ace Computers.

Anne's class visited Ace Computers.

A guide named Cliff gave them a tour.

A guide named Cliff gave them a tour.

Andy and Carl liked the computers.

Andy and Carl liked the computers.

WELCOME TO ACE
COMPUTER COMPANY

Writing Cursive E and O

Cursive **E** looks a little like manuscript **E**. You can see manuscript **O** in cursive **O**. Trace and write the letters.

Trace and write the proper nouns. Always join **E** to the letter that follows it, but do not join **O**.

Eugene, Oregon

Eugene, Oregon

Elsa

Elsa

Oliver

Oliver

82

Trace and write the sentences.

Open the program.

Open the program.

Olivia pressed Enter to begin.

Olivia pressed Enter to begin.

Otis and Eddie share computer E.

Otis and Eddie share computer E.

83

Practice

Write the letters.

$\mathcal{A}$
$\mathcal{C}$
$\mathcal{E}$
$\mathcal{O}$

$\mathcal{A}$
$\mathcal{C}$
$\mathcal{E}$
$\mathcal{O}$

Circle your best letter in each line.

Write the names of these places.

America

Canada

Alaska

California

Ohio

East Coast

Europe

Orient

84

Review

The computer screen shows the names of the students in Mrs. Olsen's class. Write their names in cursive.

Class List

Carl   Emily
Arlene Otto
Oscar   Adam
Ellen   Carrie

Carl

Emily

Arlene

Otto

Oscar

Adam

Ellen

Carrie

Evaluation

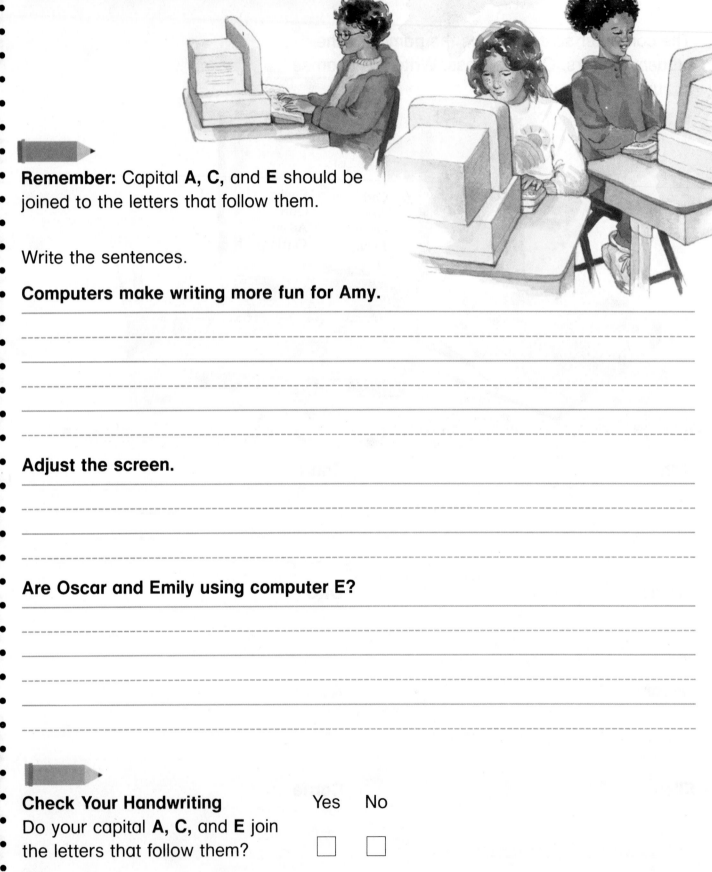

Remember: Capital **A, C,** and **E** should be joined to the letters that follow them.

Write the sentences.

Computers make writing more fun for Amy.

_____

- -

- -

- -

Adjust the screen.

_____

- -

- -

Are Oscar and Emily using computer E?

_____

- -

- -

- -

Check Your Handwriting

Do your capital **A, C,** and **E** join
the letters that follow them?

Yes   No

☐   ☐

Letter, Word, and Sentence Spacing

There should be more space between words than between letters in a word. There should be more space between sentences than between words.

Be careful to space your writing so your tall letters do not run into your descenders. Write the sentences. After each sentence, answer the question.

Arnold plays games on the computer.

Did you use the correct letter spacing?   Yes ☐   No ☐

Aunt Effie uses a computer at work.

Did you use the correct word spacing?   Yes ☐   No ☐

Computers are common. Offices and stores use them.

Did you use the correct sentence spacing?   Yes ☐   No ☐

Writing Cursive H and K

You can see manuscript **H** and **K** in cursive **H** and **K**.
Trace and write the letters.

Trace and write the names of the cities and states.
Join **K** to the letter that follows it, but do not join **H**.

Hi Hat, Kentucky

Hi Hat, Kentucky

Kansas City, Kansas

Kansas City, Kansas

Trace and write the sentences.

Kristy's family went to Kentucky.

Kristy's family went to Kentucky.

Historic sights were seen in Harrodsburg.

Historic sights were seen in Harrodsburg.

Horses were Kristy's favorite sight.

Horses were Kristy's favorite sight.

Writing Cursive N, M, and U

Cursive **N** and **M** look a little like manuscript **N** and **M**. Cursive **U** looks very much like manuscript **U**.
Trace and write the letters.

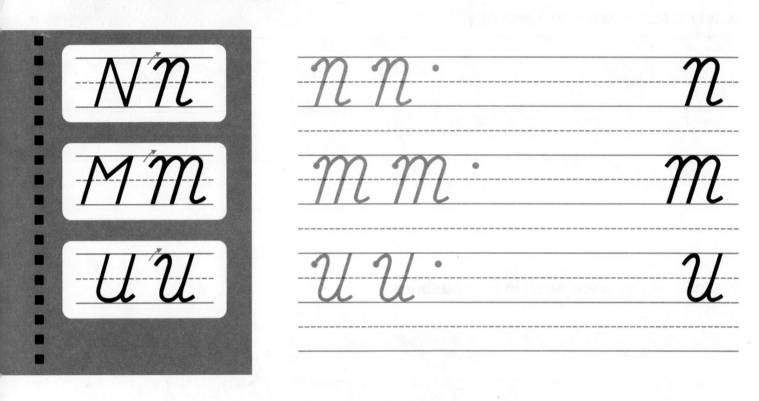

Trace and write the names of the cities and states.
Always join **N, M,** and **U** to the letters that follow them.

Navajo, New Mexico

Navajo, New Mexico

Neely, Mississippi

Neely, Mississippi

Trace and write the sentences.

Neal and Maria visit their family in Utah.

Neal and Maria visit their family in Utah.

Maria loves riding horses with Uncle Ned.

Maria loves riding horses with Uncle Ned.

Neal likes to fish with Uncle Mark.

Neal likes to fish with Uncle Mark.

Writing Cursive V, W, and Y

Cursive **V**, **W**, and **Y** look a little like manuscript **V**, **W**, and **Y**. Trace and write the letters.

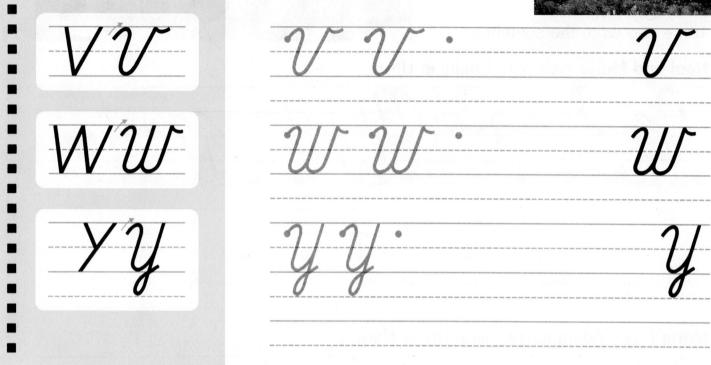

Trace and write the names of the cities and states. Remember to join cursive **Y** to the letter that follows it, but do not join **V** or **W**.

Yakima, Washington

Yakima, Washington

Van, West Virginia

Van, West Virginia

Trace and write the sentences.

Valerie and Wendy go to national parks.

Valerie and Wendy go to national parks.

Wednesday they left for Yellowstone.

Wednesday they left for Yellowstone.

Valerie's favorite park is Yosemite.

Valerie's favorite park is Yosemite.

Practice

Write the letters.

$\mathcal{H}$ $\mathcal{H}$

$\mathcal{K}$ $\mathcal{K}$

$\mathcal{N}$ $\mathcal{N}$

$\mathcal{M}$ $\mathcal{M}$

$\mathcal{U}$ $\mathcal{U}$

$\mathcal{V}$ $\mathcal{V}$

$\mathcal{W}$ $\mathcal{W}$

$\mathcal{Y}$ $\mathcal{Y}$

Circle your best letter in each line.

Write the sentence.

Walter Young visited Uncle Ken in Montpelier, Vermont.

Review

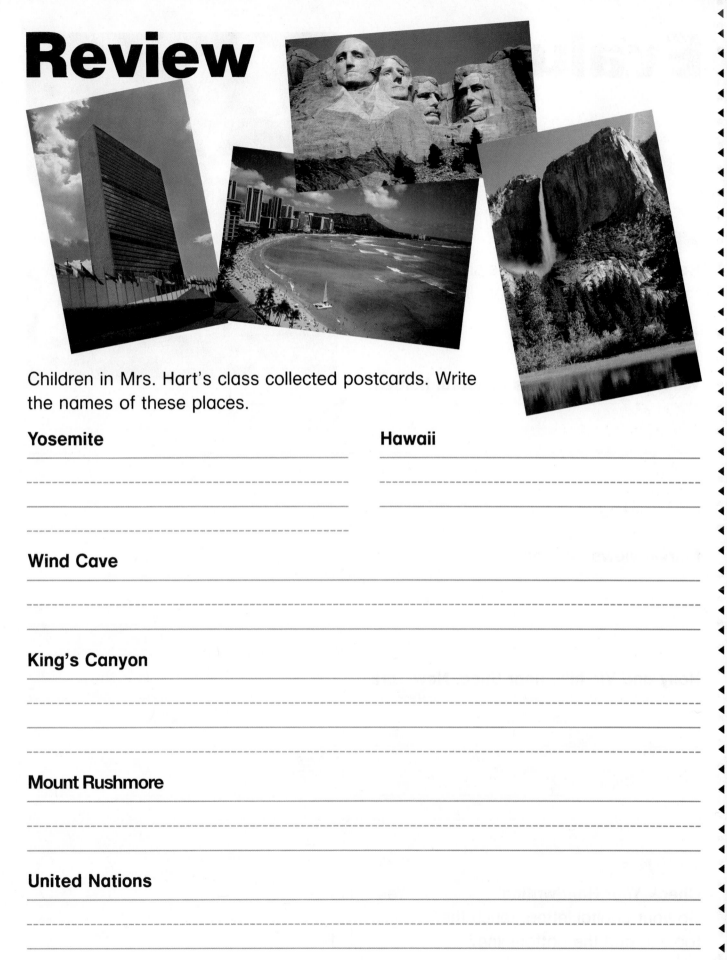

Children in Mrs. Hart's class collected postcards. Write the names of these places.

Yosemite

Hawaii

Wind Cave

King's Canyon

Mount Rushmore

United Nations

Evaluation

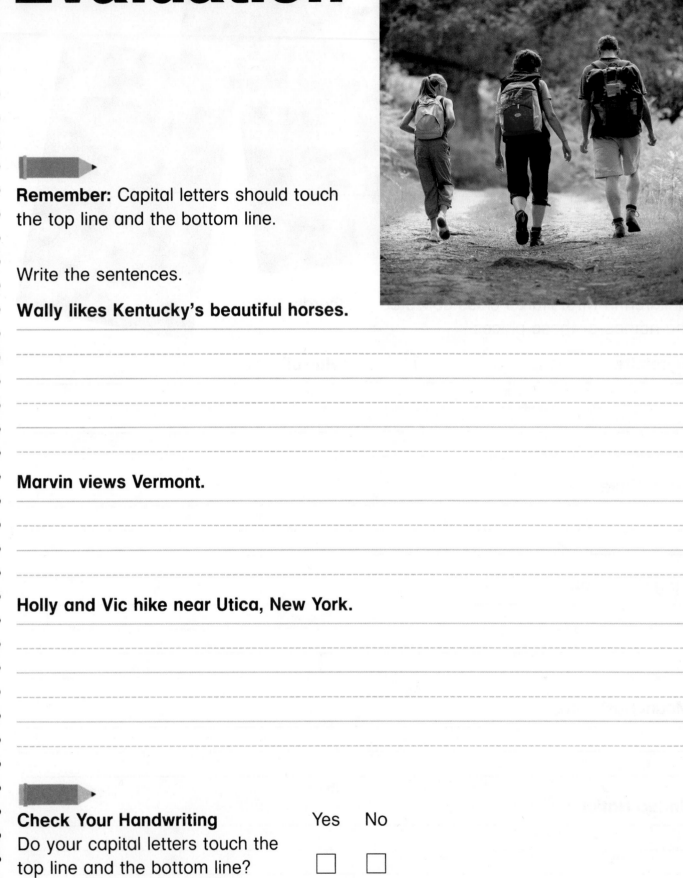

Remember: Capital letters should touch the top line and the bottom line.

Write the sentences.

Wally likes Kentucky's beautiful horses.

Marvin views Vermont.

Holly and Vic hike near Utica, New York.

Check Your Handwriting

Do your capital letters touch the top line and the bottom line?

Yes   No

☐   ☐

Writing a Thank-you Note

Neal wrote a thank-you note to his Uncle Mark when he and his family returned home.

Copy Neal's note on the lines below. Be sure to line up the date and the closing of the note. Make sure you space your words evenly. Try not to let your tall letters touch your descenders as you write.

date —┐

*July 26, 200_*

Hi Uncle Mark,
  We had a wonderful time visiting you in Utah. We want to thank you very much.

    Your nephew,
  Neal

closing —

Addressing an Envelope

Neal looked up Uncle Mark's address. Then he addressed the envelope. Notice that Neal did not address the envelope to "Uncle Mark." Use a person's real name on the envelope.

Neal put his return address in the upper left corner of the envelope. When you write an address, remember to use all capital manuscript letters and no punctuation marks. Abbreviate words like *Street* and *Avenue*, and the name of the state.

Copy the addresses on the envelope below. Remember to form your letters clearly and keep your lines straight.

NEAL KOEHLER
609 HAMILTON ST
OMAHA NE 68104

MR. MARK NOVAK
703 WOODLAND AVE
CEDAR VALLEY UT 84013

Writing a Math Test

Good handwriting helps you do well on a math test. Good handwriting makes your numbers and words easy to read.

Getting Ready

- Write your name neatly on your paper.
- Read the test questions carefully.
- Be sure you understand what the questions are asking you to do.

Using Tally Charts

Tally charts help you count things.

- Each tally mark stands for one item.
- Tally charts need labels to show what you are counting.
- Use your best handwriting so your tally chart is easy to read.
  Letters and numbers should be evenly spaced.
  Letters and numbers should slant the same way.

What does the question ask me to find out?

What does this tally chart tell you?

Mrs. Hunt's Class

Boys	Girls
ⱧⱧⱧ ⱧⱧⱧ	ⱧⱧⱧ ///

There are 10 boys and 8 girls in Mrs. Hunt's class.

- If you make a mistake, fix it as your teacher tells you.
  Which should you do?
  Draw a line through it and rewrite it. ☐
  Erase it carefully and rewrite it. ☐

Louis completed the math test item below.

Name *Louis*

Carla's Change

Quarters	Dimes	Nickels	Pennies
//	ЖⅠ	////	ЖⅠ ЖⅠ /

Does Carla have enough money to buy a pen that costs $1.25?
If so, how much will she have left over? If not, how much more
money does she need?

Carla has $1.31 which is enough to buy the pen. She would have ~~have~~ 6 cents left over.

Look at how Louis answered the question.

	Yes	No
• Do his letters and numbers slant the same way?	☐	☐
• Are his letters and numbers evenly spaced?	☐	☐
• Is his handwriting easy to read?	☐	☐
• Did he fix mistakes carefully?	☐	☐

Which letters or numbers do not have the correct slant?
Circle them.

Which words have incorrect spacing? Draw a line under them.

Now you answer this math test question.

Jason's Change

Quarters	Dimes	Nickels	Pennies
///	/	//	++++ ++++

1. This tally chart shows how much change Jason has in his pocket. Does he have enough money to buy a bottle of juice that costs $1.00? If so, how much will he have left over? If not, how much more money does he need?

Check your handwriting.   Yes   No
- Do your letters and numbers slant
  the same way?   ☐   ☐
- Are your letters and numbers evenly spaced?   ☐   ☐
- Is your handwriting easy to read?   ☐   ☐
- Did you fix mistakes carefully?   ☐   ☐

Circle the word in your answer that shows your best handwriting.

Writing Cursive T and F

Cursive **T** and **F** look a little like manuscript **T** and **F**.
Trace and write the letters.

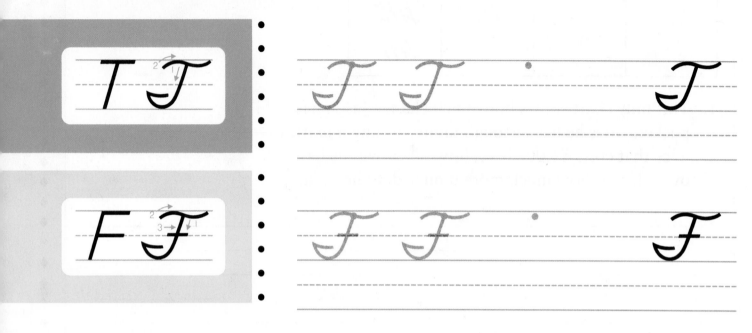

Trace and write the proper nouns. **T** and **F** are not
joined to the letters that follow them.

Tallahassee, Florida

Tallahassee, Florida

Tina

Tina

Frank

Frank

Trace and write the sentences.

The Taylors started to recycle in February.

The Taylors started to recycle in February.

Trash day is Friday.

Trash day is Friday.

Tuesday is Trenton's day for bottle pickup.

Tuesday is Trenton's day for bottle pickup.

103

Writing Cursive B, P, and R

Cursive **B**, **P**, and **R** look like manuscript **B**, **P**, and **R**. Trace and write the letters.

Trace and write the names. Do not join **B** and **P** to the letters that follow them. Always join **R** to the letter that follows it.

Brian

Brian

Paul

Paul

Rita

Rita

Beth

Beth

Trace and write the words in the sign.

Brown's Recycling
and Trash Center
Recycle Paper Products
and Bottles

Practice

Write the letters.

T F B P R

T F B P R

Circle your best letter in each line.

Write the names of the cities and states.

Paint Rock, Texas

Boca Raton, Florida

Franklin, Tennessee

Berwick, Pennsylvania

106

Review

Write the names and sentences.

Fran

Rick

Bicycling is Ron's way to save energy.

Plant a tree, Terry.

Turn off the water, Flo.

Evaluation

Remember: Leave enough space between words.

Write the sentences.

Bring home your lunch bag, Frannie.

_____

_____

_____

Reuse paper, Patty.

_____

_____

Ted and Barb pick up cans on Fridays.

_____

_____

_____

Check Your Handwriting   Yes   No
Did you leave enough space between words?   ☐   ☐

Writing Punctuation Marks

A question is a sentence that asks something. It begins with a capital letter and ends with a **question mark.**
Trace and write the question marks.

? ? ?

Sentences that show strong feelings are exclamations. They end with **exclamation marks.** Trace and write the exclamation marks.

! ! !

Quotation marks are used to show a speaker's exact words. Notice that the quotation marks at the beginning of a sentence go in a different direction from the quotation marks at the end. Trace and write the quotation marks.

"   "   "   *"   "   "*

Copy the following sentences. Be sure to slant all the punctuation marks the same way you slant your letters.

"What a mess!" said Ana. "Who can help?"

Writing a Telephone Message

Sometimes you answer the phone for someone else. You may have to take a message. Look at the message Brittany wrote for her brother Ryan. It gives all the important information. The message is neat and clearly written.

Brittany's paper does not have middle lines. Imagine a middle line as you write to help you keep your letters the correct size. Copy Brittany's telephone message on the lines below.

Telephone Message

To: *Ryan,*

Message: *Mrs. Morrow called at 8:00 P.M. The scouts will meet at Elm Park tomorrow at 10:00 A.M. to collect bottles. Please call her at 555-1789 if you can't be there.*

From: *Brittany*

Telephone Message

To:

Message:

From:

Writing Abbreviations

An abbreviation is a shortened form of a word. Abbreviations are useful when writing signs, posters, letters, and messages. Abbreviations begin with a capital letter and end with a period. Look at the dates and names below.

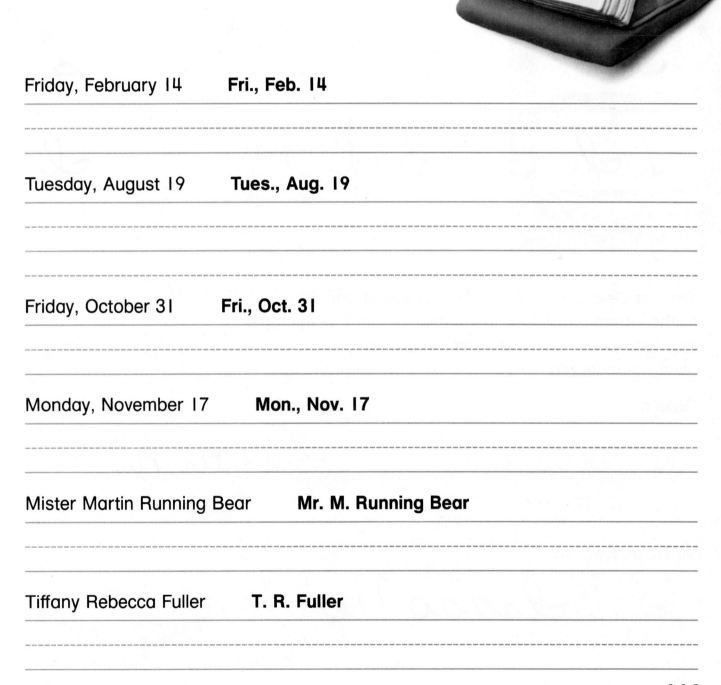

Write just the abbreviations in cursive handwriting. Be sure your letters and numbers slant the same way.

Friday, February 14   **Fri., Feb. 14**

Tuesday, August 19   **Tues., Aug. 19**

Friday, October 31   **Fri., Oct. 31**

Monday, November 17   **Mon., Nov. 17**

Mister Martin Running Bear   **Mr. M. Running Bear**

Tiffany Rebecca Fuller   **T. R. Fuller**

Writing Cursive G, S, and I

Cursive **G**, **S**, and **I** do not look like manuscript **G**, **S**, and **I**. Trace and write the letters.

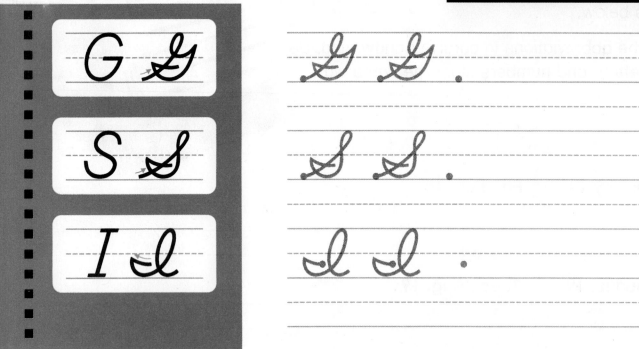

Trace and write the names. Do not join **G** and **S** to the letters that follow them. Always join **I** to the letter that follows it. Remember that the pronoun **I** is always capitalized.

Galileo

Galileo

Gemini

Gemini

Sir Isaac Newton

Sir Isaac Newton

Trace and write the sentences.

Gloria and Ingrid studied the planets.

Gloria and Ingrid studied the planets.

Sarah and I reported on Saturn's rings.

Sarah and I reported on Saturn's rings.

Spaceships interested both Greg and Ivan.

Spaceships interested both Greg and Ivan.

Writing Cursive Q, Z, and D

Cursive **Q** and **Z** do not look like manuscript **Q** and **Z**.
Cursive **D** looks something like manuscript **D**. Trace
and write the letters.

Trace and write names of the constellations. Always
join cursive **Q** and **Z** to the letters that follow them,
but do not join cursive **D**.

Dorado

Dorado

Draco

Draco

Several students in Mr. Dennison's class wrote a report about the Space Shuttle *Discovery*. They all signed their names under the title. Trace and write the title and the names.

Space Shuttle Discovery
Zack   Quan
Debbie   Zoe
Zelda   Diana
Dick   Quinn

Space Shuttle
Discovery
Zack   Quan
Debbie   Zoe
Zelda   Diana
Dick   Quinn

Writing Cursive J, X, and L

Cursive **J** does not look like manuscript **J.** You can see cursive **X** in manuscript **X.** Cursive **L** looks something like manuscript **L.** Trace and write the letters.

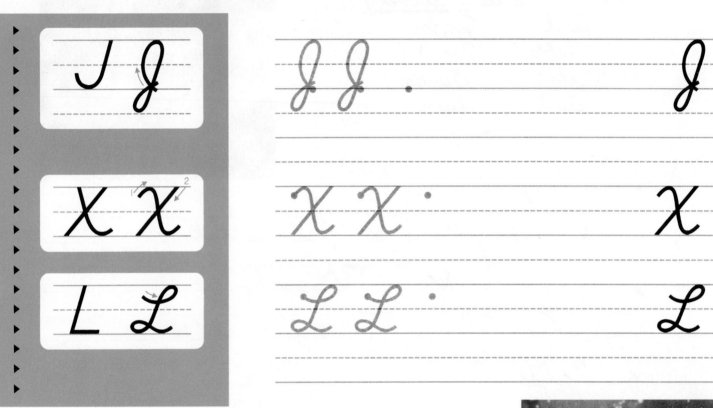

Trace and write the sentence. Always join **J** and **L** to the letters that follow them, but do not join **X.**

Jim Lovell was a Gemini astronaut.

Jim Lovell was a Gemini astronaut.

Trace and write the sentences.

X-ray telescopes can help astronomers.

X-ray telescopes can help astronomers.

Jupiter is the largest planet.

Jupiter is the largest planet.

Libra is a constellation.

Libra is a constellation.

Practice

Write the letters.

[handwriting practice lines with cursive letters G, S, I, 2, 3, D, X, L]

Circle your best letter in each line.

Write the name.

Goddard Space Flight Center

Review

Write the names.

Gail

Sue

Ira

Xavier

Louis

Dana

Jenny

Quincy

Zack

Evaluation

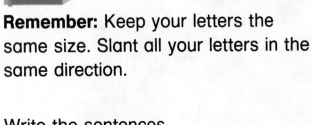

Remember: Keep your letters the same size. Slant all your letters in the same direction.

Write the sentences.

Did you visit the Johnson Space Center?

Quinn, Zoe, and Inez studied X-ray stars.

Larry and Ginny are studying Saturn.

Check Your Handwriting

Are your letters the same size?

Do your letters slant in the same direction?

Yes No
☐   ☐
☐   ☐

Writing Names of Planets

The names of the planets are proper nouns. They begin with capital letters. Write the names of the planets in cursive. Try not to let your tall letters touch your descenders.

1. _____

2. _____

3. _____

4. _____

5. _____

6. _____

7. _____

8. _____

9. _____

Write the sentence.

The sun, planets, and moons make up the solar system.

_____

_____

_____

_____

Making a Chart

Children in Mrs. Esposito's class were very interested in the astronauts. They studied the Mercury, Gemini, Apollo, and Space Shuttle astronauts. Then they made a chart of important dates in space.

Look at their chart on the next page. Copy the chart in manuscript handwriting on the form below. Be sure to adjust the size of your handwriting to fit the space.

Important Dates in Space

Important Dates in Space

Date	Event
May 5, 1961	Alan Shepard is the first American in space.
Feb. 20, 1962	John Glenn is the first American to orbit Earth.
July 20, 1969	Neil Armstrong and Edwin Aldrin are the first to land on the moon.
June 18, 1983	Sally Ride is the first American woman in space.
Aug. 30, 1983	Guion S. Bluford, Jr. is the first African American in space.
April 24, 1990	The Hubble Space Telescope is the first telescope launched in space.
Nov. 2, 2000	American William Shepherd and his crew are the first to live aboard the International Space Station.

Signing an Autograph Book

Sometimes you write on paper that has no lines at all.
Then you have to be careful to keep your lines of
handwriting straight. Make sure you leave enough
space between your letters and words.

Copy one of the rhymes in the autograph book below.
Remember to sign your name below the rhyme.

RHYMES...

East is East.
West is West.
This is the verse
That I like best.

I am no astronaut,
I have no fame,
But just the same
I'll sign my name.

Writing a Language Arts Test

Good handwriting helps you do well on language arts tests.
Good handwriting makes your written answers easy to read.
Good handwriting helps you communicate your ideas more clearly.

Getting Ready
- Read the prompt carefully.
- Think about what the prompt asks you to do.
- Think about what you want to write.

Using Capital Letters
- Use capital letters in the correct places.
  All sentences begin with capital letters.
  Capital letters are also used to begin proper nouns,
  abbreviations, titles, and initials.
- Use your best handwriting.
  Capital letters should be larger than lower-case letters.
  Capital letters should touch the top and bottom lines.

June 4, 20___

Dear Bill,

- Review and edit your writing.
  Use proofreading marks to
  make corrections or erase
  carefully and rewrite.

Proofreading Marks
Use these marks to edit your work.

⌤   New paragraph

≡   Capital letter

/   Lowercase letter

◯   Correct the spelling.

∧   Add something.

   Remove something.

Here is a writing prompt and Mika's answer.

Write a thank-you note to a friend or family member for
something nice that person has done for you.

October 9, 20___

Dear Aunt judy,
    Thank you for the
new ~~new~~ harry potter book
you sent me. It arrived
on monday and I
finished it on thursday.
you always choose
excellent books for me
                Love,
                Mika

Look at how Mika wrote her note.   Yes   No
- Did she use capital letters at the
  beginning of all sentences?   ☐   ☐
- Did she use capital letters for all proper nouns?   ☐   ☐
- Do all her capital letters touch the top and
  bottom lines?   ☐   ☐
- Did she fix her all mistakes?   ☐   ☐
- Is her handwriting easy for a teacher to read?   ☐   ☐

Which words still need capital letters? Circle them.
Which capital letters are not the correct size?
Make a line under them.

Now write a thank-you note of your own. Remember to use capitals where they are needed.

Check your handwriting. Yes No
- Did you use capital letters at the beginning of all sentences? ☐ ☐
- Did you use capital letters for all proper nouns? ☐ ☐
- Do all your capital letters touch the top and bottom lines? ☐ ☐
- Did you fix your mistakes carefully? ☐ ☐
- Is your handwriting easy for a teacher to read? ☐ ☐

Put a check mark next to the sentence that shows your best handwriting.

Index